Lucky
to be a
Teacher

To my remarkable adult children, David and Dawn, whose lives have so deeply enriched mine (they are the two extraordinary individuals I would want in my life, even if I were not related to them!)

To my charming, intelligent, and supportive husband, Raleigh (with whom I am crazy in love), and to our dear sons, Mike and Dave, who have made a place for me in their lives.

To my precious and inimitable grandchildren Cereese, Aryanna, Elise, Nash, Hunter, Brianna, and Corey, who keep me on my toes, make me laugh out loud, remind me of the family history I helped to create, and who, each in his or her own way, make me a better person.

And to the throng of children and adults I have taught for the past thirty-five years in the public schools and at the universities who give meaning, direction, and joy to my life as a teacher, mentor, coach, and friend.

Lucky
to be a
Teacher

Life-Changing Affirmations
for Positive Classrooms

Second Edition of
Cognitive Nourishment

LOUISE A. CHICKIE-WOLFE

CORWIN
A SAGE Company

For information:

Corwin
A SAGE Company
2455 Teller Road
Thousand Oaks, California 91320
(800) 233-9936
Fax: (800) 417-2466
www.corwinpress.com

SAGE Ltd.
1 Oliver's Yard
55 City Road
London EC1Y 1SP
United Kingdom

SAGE India Pvt. Ltd.
B 1/I 1 Mohan Cooperative
  Industrial Area
Mathura Road, New Delhi
India 110 044

SAGE Asia-Pacific Pte. Ltd.
33 Pekin Street #02-01
Far East Square
Singapore 048763

Printed in the United States of America

Library of Congress Cataloging-in-Publication Data

Chickie-Wolfe, Louise A.
Lucky to be a teacher : life-changing affirmations for positive classrooms / Louise A.
    Chickie-Wolfe. — 2nd ed.
        p. cm.
Rev. ed. of: Cognitive nourishment. c2005.
Includes bibliographical references.
ISBN 978-1-4129-7262-8 (pbk.)
    1. Education—Quotations, maxims, etc. 2. Affirmations. I. Chickie-Wolfe, Louise
A. Cognitive nourishment. II. Title.

PN6084.E38C48 2009
370—dc22   2009007998

This book is printed on acid-free paper.

09   10   11   12   13   10   9   8   7   6   5   4   3   2   1

Acquisitions Editor:	Carol Chambers Collins
Editorial Assistant:	Brett Ory
Production Editor:	Veronica Stapleton
Copy Editor:	Adam Dunham
Typesetter:	C&M Digitals (P) Ltd.
Proofreader:	Dennis W. Webb
Cover Designer:	Karine Hovsepian

Contents

Preface

When I first created this work, I titled it *Lucky to Be a Teacher.* It reflected my concern that too many teachers lose track of the reasons why they entered the profession and easily become frustrated by the oftentimes overwhelming responsibilities of a classroom teacher. The statistics bear this out. Data for the United States indicate that about 15% of new teachers leave teaching within the first year, 30% within three years, and 40 to 50% within five years (Smith & Ingersoll, 2003). In inner city schools, that number jumps to one half of the teachers quitting within three years (Dickson, 2006).

The first version of the book was self-published in 1994, while I was on a sabbatical leave from teaching to work on my PhD at Vanderbilt University. That sabbatical leave was to be my first of two departures from the classroom. The second departure came after I earned that degree, gave up my classroom teaching position, and became an educational and behavioral consultant. On both occasions when I left the classroom, I became acutely aware that I longed for the life-changing interactions, the shaping time, and the joy that teaching affords. As a result, I returned to the classroom after each hiatus.

The purpose for my writing the original book was to prevent the burnout that I believed took many fine teachers away from our profession.

The second version of the book was published in 2005, when Eric Jensen noticed the work and asked me to revise it for his Brain Store collection. Its name was changed to *Cognitive Nourishment: Life-Changing Affirmations for the Savvy Teacher* in order to emphasize the exciting new research that was fast emerging in the field of brain-compatible teaching, neuropsychology, and neurology.

And, now we have arrived at the third version, which you are reading. In 2006, the Brain Store was sold to Corwin Press, and I was contacted to update and revise the book. With each version, there have been changes to the book's format and content. It has now evolved into a workbook, in which is included a series of thoughtful questions after each affirmation and elaboration, personalizing the message so that teachers can apply each statement to their own unique situation.

The original goal for writing the book has not changed: to inspire teachers of every grade and ability level to refocus on the importance of their profession and to help them build the necessary resilience to stay in the field. However, the format has again evolved to get the reader more actively involved with the message through reflective contemplation and self-awareness. In my classroom, I refer to this as *self smart* or *intrapersonal work*. I tell my students that most children and many adults ignore this most important aspect of their intellectual and emotional development, yet so much can be learned from self-evaluation and healthy introspection.

It is my hope that you will face your students with renewed vigor, improved skills, and increased enthusiasm after using this workbook, that you will experience the passion and rewards that teaching can bring, and that you will fully realize that you are incredibly lucky to be a teacher!

Whereas some teachers just *hope* for positive life changes, those who use cognitive affirmations become inspired to *produce* their own future. The savvy teacher knows that a daily dose of cognitive affirmations will nourish the brain and cause it to flourish.

Think positively, work hard, and be honest as you reflect on the affirmations, and you will find new excitement and success in teaching. Remember: We tend to become the person our thoughts prepare us to be.

Acknowledgments

I wish to thank several individuals who helped in various ways during the original writing of this book in 1994, while I was earning a PhD at Vanderbilt University in Nashville, Tennessee. My fellow doctoral student and friend, Wendy Locke, strongly urged me to complete this task. The Vandy secretaries in the MRL building spent their lunch hours teaching me to line dance away my incredible stressors, ensuring my survival. Then, there was the amazing, nameless gal who worked in the library. After noticing my exhausting frustrations night after night, she took me by the hand to the archive shelves and declared, "This is what you are working so hard to accomplish. Your dissertation will live on in this university long after you are gone." Additionally, I want to thank the School Town of Munster, Indiana, who granted me a sabbatical leave of absence during which time I wrote and published the original work.

Many thanks go out to Eric Jensen, who published the book under its new title, *Cognitive Nourishment: Life-Changing Affirmations for the Savvy Teacher,* and to the capable Corwin editors, Carol Chambers Collins and assistant Brett Ory, Veronica Stapleton, and Adam Dunham.

Several other extremely important individuals helped me during the writing of this second edition. Words cannot express my appreciation for *all* that my husband, Raleigh Wolfe, did and continues to do to support me, including turning down the TV so that I can think. The loving and emotional support that my children, David and Dawn, provided during all editions of this book are too numerous to list here. They are my biggest fans and my greatest inspiration.

I want to thank my extraordinary friends and colleagues, Sue Lazar, Ginny Harvey, and Shannon O'Brien, for their many hours of stimulating conversations about teaching. That being said, this book was written because of the hundreds of caring teachers, students, and their families *from whom I learned it all*, at NISEC, Hammond, Westlake, Lake Central, and Munster, Indiana.

To everyone who helped, I genuinely thank you for supporting me, igniting my passion, and making me lucky to be a teacher.

About the Author

In 2008, **Louise A. Chickie-Wolfe** retired from classroom teaching after 35 years of experience. She taught regular education, gifted children, and students with serious learning and behavioral problems. Her experience covers elementary, middle school, high school, and college levels. Louise has also informed, inspired, and motivated educators and parents at workshops across the country. She currently serves as an adjunct professor in the Graduate School of Education at Purdue University Calumet where she has worked for more than 30 years. She earned her doctorate degree at George Peabody College of Vanderbilt University in Special Education and Human Development. She trained and supervised student teachers at Peabody College where she also taught courses in special education and managing academic and social behavior in the classroom. Named Outstanding Teacher of the Year by the Indiana chapter of the Council for Exceptional Children and again by the Inland Steel/Ryerson Foundation, Louise was also named The *Times* 2008 Woman of Merit, received a Master Teacher Endowment, and spoke at the International School Psychology Association's 2007 Colloquium in Tempere, Finland. In that same year, she received a grant to create and sponsor a junior historical society in her community for students in Grades 5, 6, 7, and 8, which keeps her busy and maintains her involvement with students. She is the coauthor of the book *Fostering Independent Learning* and coauthored a chapter in *Best Practices in School Psychology V* on study skills. She is the educational and behavioral consultant and speaker/trainer for Schoolhouse Treasures Ink, Inc., and can be reached at schoolhousetreasuresink @comcast.net.

Through these varied experiences and with the love of her family and friends, Louise has developed a teaching and personal philosophy that is positive, sensitive, and highly successful.

Louise lives in Munster, Indiana, with her husband, Raleigh. She is an adjunct professor and travels across the country eagerly sharing her expertise with teachers, psychologists, administrators, and parents. When not working, she loves completing jigsaw puzzles, walking with friends, listening to music and singing, skating, and visiting her children and grandchildren in Bothell, Washington, New York City, and Atlanta, Georgia.

Introduction

This powerful workbook is for all people who teach. The affirmations are written in first person so that teachers can read these statements and apply the ideas to their own particular teaching situations. The affirmations apply equally to male and female teachers and to all areas and levels of teaching. The contents of this workbook represent a dynamic philosophy of teaching that took 30 years of academic learning, passion, reflection, and experience to develop.

Throughout my career, I have been on the lookout for meaningful "pieces of the puzzle." The conundrum was how to reach each individual student and how to help her or him find success regardless of her or his unique challenges, limitations, or circumstances. I always felt that those pieces to the puzzle did not lie solely in the field of education. It seemed to me that the questions teachers faced were too vast to be answered in isolation and separate from other important fields of study. Therefore, I pursued learning in the related fields of psychology, sociology, neurology, and health. I became interested in many things. I searched for answers about how to motivate students, how to help them improve their own behavior, how to help families support their children, how the brain actually works when learning takes place (so that I could better understand deviations from normal), and how to teach students to study and learn efficiently and to become less dependent upon adults (teachers and parents) and to own responsibility for their actions.

Many of the answers I found in my pursuit of learning are important pieces of the puzzle. These life-changing pieces are woven into the fabric of this workbook. Using the affirmations, elaborations, and guided reflections in this workbook will take teachers on a journey of learning, discovery, and growth as they too pursue answers to the critical questions teachers face each day.

The Power of Positivity

Research indicates that people who make repeated cognitive affirmations can actually change the way their brains function. Both the positive and negative messages we tell ourselves influence our own physiology and change the actual size and connections in the brain (Foss, 1995). Additionally, what we think determines how we feel, which in turn influences how we behave. I often tell teachers that if they want to change the way a student behaves, they must first change the way that student thinks. This is also true of adults.

We are surrounded by reminders of the belief that optimism is preferable to pessimism. Most people would agree that it is better to have a positive attitude than a negative one. That being said, I'm sure you know individuals who not only appear to see the world as half empty but seem to surround themselves with others who share that point of view. Often, these people are called toxic, and we are encouraged to carefully remove ourselves from their presence whenever possible. The reason for doing so is that their negativism is contagious and will wear us down. Sometimes, we enter into relationships with these negative people in our private lives believing that we can change them significantly. Unfortunately, this is not easily accomplished, and too often we are the ones who struggle to maintain a mentally healthy outlook. However, for some of us, being around negative people is sometimes the nature of our job as we attempt to bring about a positive behavior change on behalf of students and their families. Therefore, it becomes vital for teachers to present information in such a way as to entice others into seeing their world in more positive terms.

Wikipedia, the electronic encyclopedia, offers this definition of a positive mental attitude:

> Positive mental attitude, or PMA, is a psychological term which describes a mental phenomenon in which the central idea is that one can increase achievement through optimistic thought processes. PMA implies that one has a vision of good natured change in one's mind; it employs a state of mind that continues to seek, find and execute ways to win, or find a desirable outcome, regardless of the circumstances. It rejects negativity, defeatism and hopelessness. Part of the process of achieving PMA employs motivating "self talk" and deliberate goal-directed thinking. (Wikipedia)

Emile Coue, the 19th-century and early 20th-century French professor, became a pioneer of affirmation techniques with his famous affirmation, "Every day in every way I am getting better and better" (Coue, 1923). The results of his work suggest that affirmations are powerful tools that can bring about major changes in the subconscious mind. Brain research indicates that affirmations can reset the brain through suggestions and that the brain processes suggestions or affirmations as being real. This inner speech serves as the principle vehicle of thought and self-direction (Brown, 2003). The use of positive thoughts in the form of affirmations as part of a treatment plan can even improve our health, as in the case of breast cancer (Spiegel, 1991) and fibromyalgia (Peterson, 2005). It has also been used successfully in couples' therapy (Palisi, 1992).

Focusing on teachers and students, Bandura (1997) researched this philosophy and concluded that those who believed in themselves had what he called "efficacy" and were more successful than those who sat around and waited for luck to bring them success.

We know that mental practice actually improves performance. We see it at the Olympics where athletes close their eyes and visualize their events before they occur, going through the phases of their performance in their minds eye before they actually perform them. In essence, they have won the competition in their mind before they actually compete. Athletes from a variety of sports have benefited from this type of visual imagery and mental rehearsal (Plessinger, 2008; Martin & Hall, 1995; Pavio, 1985; Roure et al. 1998).

Others outside of athletics have discovered the power of positive thinking. In a prisoner of war camp in North Vietnam, Air Force Colonel George Robert Hall was locked in a small cell for seven years. Every day, Hall played an entire game of golf in his imagination as a way of maintaining his sanity, even under extremely harsh conditions. Upon his release, his golf game had actually improved (Power-Of-Imagination, 2007). The power of the mind to practice something repeatedly and with concentration and positive emotions can bring about amazing improvements. In this same way, the affirmations in this workbook will actually become a part of you if you consistently and persistently practice them.

A Positive Mindset in the Classroom

Carol Dweck (2006), in her book *Mindset: The New Psychology of Success,* describes a growth mindset where everyone can change and grow through application and experience. She feels the view you adopt for yourself profoundly affects the way you lead your life.

Similarly, teachers can use a positive mindset to establish a climate for their students that sets the stage for good behavior. For example, before children with behavior problems go out for recess, if they are verbally reminded to play fairly with others, those positive thoughts that are brought into their minds increase the likelihood that they will have successful interactions with others during that unstructured time.

In my classroom, I created a large banner that said, "Your Brain Believes What You Tell It." I taught my students that thinking negative thoughts about themselves made it less likely that they would be successful. This is true in all areas of life, including academics, social interactions, developing emotional well being, during performances, and in sports. Conversely, making positive self-statements improved their chances of reaching their goals. So if a child said, "I'm going to fail this test," my students would direct his attention to the banner and remind him that he had just "programmed" his brain to perform poorly.

Cognitive affirmations nourish our thoughts and beliefs. These powerful statements are truly life changing. When repeated daily, cognitive affirmations establish a positive mindset that guides our behavior toward goal attainment.

Cognitive Affirmations

Cognitive affirmations are positive statements about your beliefs; they are self-statements, or self-talk, that influence your brain to act in a desired way, like helping you strive for excellence and reach your goals. Each affirmation in this book is followed by an elaboration, a short paragraph that explains the affirmation in more detail. Next are guided reflections that involve the reader in personalizing the affirmation to their own circumstances.

As you read this book, take the time to visually imagine the affirmations and elaborative statements as they apply to you. Try to actually see yourself putting the statements into action. Accept any statements that represent your beliefs and add any thoughts of your own that affirm your personal commitment to teaching. Directions for writing your own affirmations and blank pages at the end of the book are provided for this express purpose.

It has been a tremendous learning experience for me to formulate and describe my teaching philosophy through cognitive affirmations.

Taking the time to compose and physically write your beliefs in the form of affirmations will help you develop your own positive philosophy for teaching others.

Brain Power

The brain believes what we tell it and it reacts accordingly. Amazingly, an idea doesn't even have to be said aloud for the brain to be solidly programmed in powerful ways to believe the message. We only have to *think* about something for it to come true! This is the reason we maintain fears and phobias even when we understand that they are irrational and even when they wreak havoc with our lives. It also explains why people can experience superhuman strength when they face crisis situations.

When students think negative thoughts such as, "Oh, this is horrible! I'm going to fail this test," they decrease the likelihood of doing their best work. Programming their brain in this negative way often sabotages their performance. But telling the brain positive things can have powerful outcomes in the same way that telling the brain negative things influences it negatively (Bandura, 1997). When students make positive statements such as, "I studied hard, and I know I'm going to do a great job on this test," they increase their chances of doing just that.

In the same way, your brain will respond positively if you read the cognitive affirmations in this workbook daily and program your brain to be successful. Like the brain of a student, the brain of a teacher is strongly influenced by what it is told. With cognitive affirmations, you can turn any negative thoughts you may be having into a positive program for success and growth. This workbook will help you accomplish that goal.

Brain-Compatible Instruction

Though affirmations have been around for a long time, our understanding of how they change the neural network within the brain and our appreciation of their power within the body of knowledge in brain research is relatively new. Despite its newness, however, much research supports the fact that teachers can create an atmosphere within the classroom that invites learning through brain-compatible instruction (Jensen, 1998). Reframing self-statements through cognitive affirmations will open new neural pathways that allow us to stretch our abilities and achieve success far greater than ever imagined.

Now, teachers understand that an absence of threat allows the brain to achieve levels of higher-order thinking. Conversely, stress, anxiety, or fear immobilizes students, making it impossible for them to think clearly and effectively. The end results of threat are often academic and social failure, frustration, behavior problems, and increased drop-out rates from school. Putting the brain at ease through brain-compatible instruction can reverse this trend. Because the affirmations in this workbook are brain compatible, they are better able to help any teacher think positive thoughts about how and what they teach.

A Joyful Message for All Educators

The cognitive affirmations and subsequent elaborations in this workbook remind us of the joys and responsibilities of teaching that are often forgotten in the day-to-day demands of our profession. We are routinely asked to do more with less. Effective teaching strategies have been blended with positive affirmational statements, making this a book of methodology as well as inspiration. It is appropriate for teachers of students of all ages (preschool through college) and of all ability levels (regular, special, and gifted).

School districts will find this workbook a powerful tool for staff development. As teachers use this workbook daily, they will boost their level of confidence, enthusiasm, knowledge, awareness, and pride. It will be useful to principals, superintendents, educational specialists, counselors, social workers, school psychologists, therapists, coaches, home school teachers, mentors, tutors, school board members, student teachers, and university professors involved in teacher education programs. It is a powerful tool for anyone who teaches others in any capacity.

Workbook Procedures

This workbook will help teachers on three levels. First, thoughtfully repeating the affirmations over and over, several times each day, will be imperative to establishing a positive attitude and changing old ways of thinking. Next, carefully reading the elaboration following each affirmation will help the teacher understand the dynamics of the affirmation and all that it encompasses. This is philosophy-building time.

Third, the Guided Reflections sections of this workbook, which follow each affirmation and elaboration, put the teacher to work actively thinking about challenging ways to strengthen his or her skills, attitudes, and practices. They will improve self-awareness and increase a teacher's ability to meet the needs of a diverse population of students and their caregivers. They will stretch the teacher in new directions to excel in new areas and to achieve greater successes. They will boost teacher morale and instill a deep sense of pride in the teaching profession.

This workbook is equally beneficial for both novice and veteran teachers. It is recommended that brand new teachers focus their attention exclusively on the Affirmation and Elaboration sections in this workbook. Adequately completing the Guided Reflections can only be accomplished after experiential learning gained through actual teaching experience.

Teachers should think of the contents of this workbook in the same way they think of diet and exercise. They are all important aspects of good health that should not be neglected. Just as with diet and exercise, this workbook must be used regularly and should be built into your routine and practiced over time as a way of life. Even after you have completed your responses to the Guided Reflections, you will be amazed at how useful it is to repeat that task at a later date.

Reading 33 affirmations in a row can be overwhelming, but selecting one affirmation to concentrate on each day or for several days will enable you to use this book more effectively. Keep the book on your desk as a visual reminder to repeat a selected affirmation several times throughout the day. Doing so will keep you focused on one area of professional growth at a time. As you repeat the affirmations and read the elaborations, you will be reprogramming your brain to think positively about your profession and the ways you interact with your students and others.

It is recommended that the Guided Reflections sections be done one at a time. Do not try to complete this workbook in one sitting! These sections require a great deal of thinking and introspection. Some school principals use one affirmation, with its elaboration and guided reflection, at each faculty meeting throughout the school year to generate dynamic discussions about education and provide personalized staff development opportunities. This "food for thought" group activity is certainly how the term *cognitive nourishment* was intended in its original form.

One caution needs to be offered about how one repeats the affirmations. To this end, I would like you to try an experiment at this time. Please repeat "Elephants are not purple" five times out loud. Now repeat that phrase out loud again over and over while trying to imagine what your favorite type of pizza looks like. Stop saying "Elephants are not purple" when you can clearly see your favorite pizza with all of its toppings in your minds' eye.

Were you successful in visualizing your favorite pizza? Even while you were still repeating your elephant phrase? If so, you can easily appreciate that we have the capacity to merely repeat words *without any thinking*. We had stopped thinking about the elephant even though we were still repeating the words. Saying the affirmations without concentrating on what they mean is a similar waste of time and will yield poor, if any, results. Be sure to keep your mind on what you are saying, and let yourself react emotionally to the words as you picture yourself experiencing each affirmation.

Remember, say the words thoughtfully. For the affirmations that are new to you, say the words as though they already apply to you. For example, if you are not well organized at this time, you will say, "I am organized," and picture in your mind what that looks like. See yourself doing it now and believing in it now . . . and you will do both successfully.

Henry David Thoreau (1985/1854) wrote in *Walden*, "I know of no more encouraging fact than the unquestionable ability of man to elevate his life by a conscious endeavor" (p. 79). Making an intentional effort to repeat positive affirmations about teaching is one such endeavor that will surely bring about the success we seek as educators.

Good luck!

Affirmations, Elaborations, and Guided Reflections

Affirmation 1

I believe in the inherent worth of each student.

Elaboration

Every child committed to my care has worth and importance. My students don't have to prove that to me. I value them as human beings, and I realize that their parents have entrusted them to my care. I will treat my students just as I would want a child of my own to be treated.

Guided Reflections

I believe in the inherent worth of each student.

Focus on your most challenging student. What is the inherent worth of this student?

_____

_____

_____

_____

_____

_____

_____

_____

_____

_____

What are some of his or her positive qualities?

_____

_____

_____

_____

_____

_____

_____

_____

_____

_____

List two things you can do to help increase appreciation for life and living things within your classroom for all students.

1. _____

2. _____

How would you want a child of your own to be treated in school?

_____

_____

_____

_____

_____

_____

_____

_____

_____

_____

Affirmation 2

I make a difference in the lives of my students.

 ## Elaboration

My students remember with satisfaction the time we spend together. Each student gains in knowledge, confidence, and ability during our interactions. I take students to places of learning they have never been before. Each student benefits from our paths having crossed and looks back with pride on her or his accomplishments and growth.

Guided Reflections

I make a difference in the lives of my students.

List all the ways you know you have made a difference in the lives of your students. Consider academic, emotional, and social areas where you made a difference. Be as specific as possible. (Note: Teachers are not supposed to brag, so we often overlook or understate our actual effects on our students. Now is the time to honestly consider the differences you have made in the lives of your students.)

_____

_____

_____

_____

_____

_____

_____

_____

What are some of the happiest memories that *you* have about accomplishments your students have made both in and out of the classroom while under your guidance?

_____

_____

_____

_____

_____

_____

_____

_____

_____

_____

What are some of the lasting memories your students have about the time they spent with you?

_____

_____

_____

_____

_____

_____

_____

_____

_____

_____

_____

Affirmation 3

*I create a safe and friendly atmosphere
in my classroom.*

Elaboration

*Regardless of what my students face outside of school, they want to
be in our classroom. They know that they are important; they learn
to help one another and share the joys and frustrations of growing
up. They are brave and confident. My students know that their
opinions matter and that they are treated fairly. They build and
maintain friendships with each other and with me. We laugh and cry
and learn together, and our classroom is a magical place.*

Guided Reflections

I create a safe and friendly atmosphere in my classroom.

Reflect on some of the conditions that your students face outside of
school.

_____

_____

_____

_____

_____

_____

_____

_____

List a few of the reasons that your students want to be in your classroom.

_____

_____

_____

_____

_____

_____

_____

List ways your students have helped others.

_____

_____

_____

_____

_____

_____

_____

What additional steps can you take to ensure that each student feels safe and is treated fairly?

_____

_____

_____

_____

_____

_____

_____

_____

Affirmation 4

I smile a lot and am very positive in my work.

Elaboration

My students like being around me. They are able to count on me and reflect on school as a happy experience. Because enthusiasm and joy are contagious, they also laugh a lot and are optimistic about their future. They see that I love my work, and they love theirs.

Guided Reflections

I smile a lot and am very positive in my work.

Name three things that really make you smile (at home and in the classroom).

_____

_____

_____

_____

_____

_____

_____

_____

_____

_____

_____

In what ways do you show your students that you love your work?

_____

_____

_____

_____

_____

_____

_____

_____

_____

_____

_____

_____

List some of the words you often use to let students know you are happy to be there with them.

_____

_____

_____

_____

_____

_____

_____

_____

_____

_____

_____

_____

Affirmation 5

I say exactly what I mean and mean exactly what I say.

 Elaboration

I think carefully before I speak. I am clear and concise, and I do not make idle threats. My students are able to count on me to be predictably fair when they are behaving appropriately as well as when they are not. When they lose control, my students count on me to help them regain it. I keep my promises. I am not vague, because my students need to understand exactly what I mean. When I say it, I mean it. When I say I care about them, I do. When I say I will correct unacceptable behavior, I will. When I say my students can count on me, they can.

 Guided Reflections

I say exactly what I mean and mean exactly what I say.

When your students behave appropriately, what are the consequences?

_____

_____

_____

_____

_____

_____

_____

_____

When your students behave inappropriately, what are the consequences?

_____

_____

_____

_____

_____

Think of the last time a student misbehaved in your class. Try to write the exact words you used to respond to that behavior.

_____

_____

_____

_____

_____

Look at the statement you just wrote and decide if you were clear and concise in your response. Tell why you feel this way.

_____

_____

_____

_____

_____

What things do you do and say that show your students they can count on you?

_____

_____

_____

_____

_____

_____

Affirmation 6

I am fair and considerate of my students' feelings.

Elaboration

I treat my students fairly but not necessarily equally, for some require more assistance at times than others. I care about my students and how they feel. I speak to them in private about sensitive issues, and I understand when they are having a rough day. I respect my students and their families.

Guided Reflections

I am fair and considerate of my students' feelings.

Jot down the names of three students who require more assistance than others.

_____

_____

_____

_____

_____

_____

_____

_____

_____

_____

Brainstorm new ways of meeting their needs that take their feelings into account.

_____

_____

_____

_____

_____

_____

_____

_____

List some of the ways you can help a student who is having a rough day.

_____

_____

_____

_____

_____

_____

_____

_____

Describe a new way of connecting with the parents of your students.

_____

_____

_____

_____

_____

_____

_____

_____

Affirmation 7

I am creative and competent.

Elaboration

Although I don't know everything there is to know about education, I am well trained and capable of performing my duties effectively. Each day of a teacher's life is different from any of the others; I love this unpredictable nature of my work. I thrive on creatively teaching the same idea in novel ways. Every time I present a lesson, I improve the way I do it. I continually seek new materials, ideas, and activities for my classroom. I am thrilled each time the "lightbulb" lights for one of my students. This "A-Ha" moment brings me joy.

Guided Reflections

I am creative and competent.

Name the two areas in which you feel most competent.

_____

_____

_____

_____

_____

_____

_____

_____

_____

_____

What was the most recent unpredictable event that happened in your classroom?

_____

_____

_____

_____

_____

How did you and your students react to it?

_____

_____

_____

_____

_____

Concentrate on the last time a student had an "A-Ha" moment of understanding. Describe it.

_____

_____

_____

_____

_____

How did it make you feel?

_____

_____

_____

_____

_____

_____

_____

Affirmation 8

I realize that teaching is a profession of utmost importance.

 ## Elaboration

When I look around, I am hard-pressed to find another career that is as important to the world as teaching. I have seen many gifted teachers leave the field of teaching to find more lucrative positions, and this saddens me. I am very proud of what I do, and I realize that the future rests on my shoulders. I do not recoil from this awesome responsibility—I welcome it.

Guided Reflections

I realize that teaching is a profession of utmost importance.

List the names of two individuals that you knew who left the field of education before retirement, and give their reasons for leaving.

_____

_____

_____

_____

_____

_____

_____

_____

_____

How will you become more resilient to increase your staying power?

_____

_____

_____

_____

_____

_____

_____

_____

_____

_____

Name two aspects of your teaching of which you are very proud.

1. _____

2. _____

Focus on the future, and visualize your former students finding great success. What accomplishments are they realizing?

_____

_____

_____

_____

_____

_____

_____

_____

_____

_____

Affirmation 9

I believe that children are our most important natural resource.

Elaboration

Look around. The social problems facing this nation are horrendous: poverty, abuse, oppression, divorce, illness, illiteracy, homelessness, prejudice, drugs, crime, suicide, violence, fear, terrorism, isolation. Children are having children. Children are killing children—with no regard for the value and quality of life. Will values, morals, and spirituality become extinct? Who will put this world back in order? Who will calm the stormy seas? Who will make a difference and right the wrongs?

My students will!

Guided Reflections

I believe that children are our most important natural resource.

List some of the problems that your students face outside of class.

_____

_____

_____

_____

_____

_____

_____

In what ways do you help your students cope with their difficulties?

_____

_____

_____

_____

_____

_____

How can you help your community value and celebrate the lives of its children?

_____

_____

_____

_____

_____

_____

_____

We touch the lives of children in ways that we can never imagine. Think of the one student that you feel you have not positively affected regardless of your efforts. Now imagine that you, in fact, *did* make a difference in his or her life even though you didn't think so. Draw that student as an adult, having benefited from your guidance.

Now *smile* because you may never know how far your influence has benefited each of your students—but it has!

Affirmation 10

I am a lifelong learner, and my students know it.

⸂ Elaboration

Because I value knowledge, I model that belief in my classroom. My students see me reading to gain information and for enjoyment. I show, through example, that writing is a worthwhile skill. I use mathematics to make sense of my surroundings, and I solve problems and resolve conflicts to illustrate the importance of knowledge. I continue to seek new information about many topics, and I allow my students to join me in this exciting pursuit. I demonstrate my enthusiasm for learning new things, and I prove each day that I have many more questions than answers.

⸷ Guided Reflections

I am a lifelong learner, and my students know it.

What choices have you made that show you value knowledge?

_____

_____

_____

_____

_____

_____

_____

_____

Do your students have the opportunity to witness your enthusiasm for learning? If not, why not? If so, how?

_____

_____

_____

_____

_____

_____

_____

Name three things you'd like to learn more about.

1. _____

2. _____

3. _____

Think of the last time you learned something from your students? What was it?

_____

_____

_____

_____

_____

How did they teach it to you?

_____

_____

_____

_____

_____

_____

Affirmation 11

I am organized, and I plan ahead.

 Elaboration

I invest the time necessary to do my job well. I plan my lessons carefully and organize my materials ahead of time. I stay focused on the goals and do not become sidetracked with irrelevant tasks. I think about my students and their strengths, and I teach accordingly.

 Guided Reflections

I am organized, and I plan ahead.

On a scale of 1 to 5 (5 is the highest score), how do you rate your organizational skills at home? _____ and at school? _____

Are these scores the same? _____ If not, explain the difference.

_____

_____

_____

_____

_____

_____

_____

Think of two things you could do right away to make yourself more organized.

1. _____

2. _____

What tricks do you use to stay focused and not get sidetracked when teaching?

_____

_____

_____

_____

_____

_____

_____

_____

_____

What do you do to teach to your students' strengths?

_____

_____

_____

_____

_____

_____

_____

_____

_____

Affirmation 12

I believe that teaching is satisfying and rewarding.

Elaboration

Success is doing what you love and loving what you do. That's how I feel about teaching. Little can compare to the sense of satisfaction a teacher feels when students master concepts previously foreign to them. Every squeal that ends with "Oh, I get it!" brings a feeling of pride that is difficult to describe. Students are so uninhibited and refreshing! Warm hugs come from the little ones, with a sincere, "I love you." Pictures drawn just for me decorate my refrigerator at home. Letters and visits come from former students and are rewards few people ever enjoy. Sometimes, I am trusted enough for students to reveal their real selves to me—selves others do not often get to see. Teaching gives me a deep sense of satisfaction.

Guided Reflections

I believe that teaching is satisfying and rewarding.

In what ways are you rewarded as a teacher?

_____

_____

Name some of the ways that your students show their appreciation for all that you do.

_____

_____

In what ways have their parents shown you that your efforts are appreciated?

_____

_____

_____

Teachers are leaders—in their schools, their school districts, their communities, and in their field. Name two things you can do to become more of an educational leader in each of these categories.

School

1. _____

2. _____

District

1. _____

2. _____

Community

1. _____

2. _____

Your Field

1. _____

2. _____

Name four aspects of your work that bring you deep satisfaction.

1. _____

2. _____

3. _____

4. _____

Affirmation 13

*I am not the same teacher I was
yesterday, because each day I learn
and experience more.*

 ## Elaboration

*With the passage of time, I become more and more competent. I
discover more about myself and learn new ways of reaching children.
I am in a place today that I have never been before. I have never
known as much as I know today. Each experience adds wisdom that
I carry into my classroom and share with my students. The future
holds such promise for us all.*

 ## Guided Reflections

*I am not the same teacher I was yesterday, because each day I learn
and experience more.*

Name two recent discoveries you made about yourself.

_____

_____

_____

_____

_____

_____

_____

_____

In what ways are you more knowledgeable than ever before?

_____

_____

_____

_____

_____

If this were your last day on earth, what wisdom would you leave behind for others?

_____

_____

_____

_____

_____

If all your dreams could come true, what would the future hold?

_____

_____

_____

_____

_____

Think of one step you could take to make one of those dreams come true.

_____

_____

_____

_____

_____

_____

Affirmation 14

*I remember how much it hurts to fail,
and I am patient and understanding
with students' difficulties.*

Elaboration

When students are struggling, I am there to help them in the same way my family and friends are there to help me when things do not go well. I am sensitive to the feelings of my students. I let them know it is natural to make mistakes and to not have all the answers. I empathize with their plight and do all I can to help them overcome their frustrations or endure their pain. For some of my students, school is a frightening place where just answering a question means taking a risk for which they are ill-prepared. Others are impulsive and continually break the rules. Some cannot read well or pass tests no matter how hard they study. Many students have no friends. Whatever difficulties my students experience, I am there to assist them.

Guided Reflections

I remember how much is hurts to fail, and I am patient and understanding with students' difficulties.

Think of the last time you failed at something. What was it, and how did that make you feel?

_____

_____

_____

_____

_____

Sometimes it is helpful to put ourselves into new learning situations in order to revisit and remember the emotions associated with the struggles of a novice learner. List three important new things you could learn that would give you the opportunity to feel and understand that struggle.

1. _____

2. _____

3. _____

Select one of the above new learning tasks and commit to learning it. Which one did you choose? When and how can you begin learning it?

_____

_____

_____

_____

_____

After you begin, record your emotions and thoughts below as your brain struggles with this new learning.

_____

_____

_____

_____

_____

In what ways do you help your students emotionally prepare for new learning?

_____

_____

_____

_____

_____

Affirmation 15

I do not take personally anything said to me in anger by a student.

Elaboration

I know that remaining objective during a problem is important. I know, too, that youngsters can become upset with their teachers for a variety of reasons, many over which we have no control. When students lose control, I am there to calm them down and help them regain their composure. I remember that much of what they say at a time when they are most angry is the truth turned upside down. "I hate you, and I hate this school!" shouted in anger often means a student does care but feels somehow betrayed. I accept, with no animosity, any apology in whatever form it is given. After consequences are served by the student, I wipe the slate clean and harbor no ill-feelings. Then, I let the student know that all is forgiven and that our relationship continues unshaken.

Guided Reflections

I do not take personally anything said to me in anger by a student.

List some of the reasons you believe that students become angry at school.

_____

_____

_____

_____

_____

_____

Have you ever seen a student who arrived at school already angry? _____ What things can teachers and school staff do to assist a student in this situation?

_____

_____

_____

_____

_____

_____

Generally, when a student's anger is met by anger from an adult, the problem escalates. How do you diffuse a student's anger?

_____

_____

_____

_____

_____

_____

Who do you know that is really good at doing this? _____

Make a point to speak with that person to discuss ways of calming down a student who is upset. Be sure to compliment the student for her or his skills in this area.

_____

_____

_____

_____

_____

_____

Affirmation 16

*I am consistent and knowledgeable
in my field.*

Elaboration

*I am mindful of school rules and consistently enforce them.
Consistency yields predictability, so my students feel secure. I
continue to pursue knowledge in my respective field of education so
that I am able to provide a strong program and a valuable experience
for my students.*

Guided Reflections

I am consistent and knowledgeable in my field.

On a scale of 1 to 5 (with 5 being the highest), rate the students in your
school for their overall ability to follow school rules. _____

Are there any rules that they find difficult to follow? _____

If yes, what are they?

_____

_____

_____

_____

_____

_____

Brainstorm ways you and your colleagues can help students show respect for the rules.

_____

_____

_____

_____

_____

Think of something you should be doing more consistently at school. What is it?

_____

_____

_____

_____

_____

Problem solve ways to improve this.

_____

_____

_____

_____

_____

What are the three most valuable experiences you provide for your students?

1. _____

2. _____

3. _____

Now, smile and reflect on the good job you are doing!

Affirmation 17

I know my students' abilities, and I have realistic expectations for each of them.

 ## Elaboration

I carefully observe, monitor, assess, and interact with my students to gather information about their strengths, weaknesses, deficits, and interests. I uphold high standards that are obtainable for my students on a consistent basis. I know how and on what levels my students are functioning. I ask them to do meaningful tasks that they are capable of doing and for which they are prepared. I appreciate their limited time and avoid busy work that serves no purpose in accomplishing their goals. I "scaffold" their learning activities to stretch their ability in systematic and sequential steps. I have realistic academic and social expectations for all of my students.

 ## Guided Reflections

I know my students' abilities, and I have realistic expectations for each of them.

What things do you do early in the year to get to know your students better?

_____

_____

_____

_____

_____

List all the sources of information available to you to gain a clear picture of your students' strengths, weaknesses, deficits, and interests.

_____

_____

_____

_____

_____

_____

_____

How can you avoid "busy work" and ensure that each task and assignment is purposeful and meaningful to each of your students?

_____

_____

_____

_____

_____

_____

_____

_____

What are your social expectations of your students?

_____

_____

_____

_____

_____

_____

_____

_____

Affirmation 18

My students and I become a family.

 ## Elaboration

Just as with our own families, students in my classroom feel supported, encouraged, and cared about by their classmates and by me. We work together, all for one and one for all, cooperatively and with respect for one another. All students contribute to our classroom's success by using their strengths and sharing their talents and interests. We understand and appreciate our multiple intelligences and do not expect everyone to learn or think alike. Being made fun of, being bullied, being left out, or being gossiped about is unheard of among our classroom family. All students' opinions matter to each of us, especially when they do not match our own. Every student knows he or she is important to the well-being of the entire group. When students are absent, they are missed. Our family atmosphere gives my students a sense of belonging and an identity that sets the stage for learning.

 ## Guided Reflections

My students and I become a family.

What helps to establish a sense of family within your classroom?

_____

_____

_____

_____

_____

_____

How do students support one another in your classroom?

_____

_____

_____

_____

_____

Think of a time when one student showed the life skill of caring toward another person, student or adult. Describe it.

_____

_____

_____

_____

_____

Does each student feel valued in your school? If not, what can be done to improve this situation?

_____

_____

_____

_____

_____

How do your students know that they are important to you?

_____

_____

_____

_____

_____

Affirmation 19

I celebrate every milestone—even the smallest ones.

 Elaboration

I believe in celebration. Success doesn't come only at the end of the school year—it happens every day and should be measured and recognized one little piece at a time. I do not wait until the final result but find joy in every manifestation of growth as it occurs. This discovery inspires me to persevere and enjoy each day.

Guided Reflections

I celebrate every milestone—even the smallest ones.

List three ways you and your students celebrate learning and other important accomplishments.

1. _____

2. _____

3. _____

Don't wait until the end of the year to celebrate growth. Instead, focus on one small thing that you can celebrate today. What is it?

_____

_____

_____

_____

_____

Be sure to celebrate the small steps of those students whose progress is slower than others. Each little step toward the goal is a milestone for that student and needs to be recognized with celebration. Make a point to tell one such student about her or his good work and good progress today. List the milestone, and tell how you will acknowledge it.

Name all the things you can remember that have brought you joy in your profession.

Affirmation 20

I help my students find academic and personal success.

Elaboration

I individualize as much as possible to accommodate the wonderful diversity in my classroom. After I teach, I check for understanding before assigning work. I reteach when students do not understand. I tell and show at the same time. I demonstrate and then watch to be sure students are getting it right. I provide lots of practice, enriched opportunities, hands-on experiences, and specific feedback. I am a good listener. Working with students in this way just about guarantees their academic and personal success.

Guided Reflections

I help my students find academic and personal success.

In what ways do you individualize your instruction and your responses to your students?

_____

_____

_____

_____

_____

_____

_____

How do you help them find success?

_____

_____

_____

_____

_____

Can you think of a time when a student was trying to speak with you and you were too busy to really listen well? _____
If not, *Yea!* If so, what were the circumstances?

_____

_____

_____

_____

_____

Define good listening.

_____

_____

_____

_____

_____

List the enrichment activities you provide in your classroom of which you are most proud.

_____

_____

_____

_____

_____

Affirmation 21

I model honesty and dependability.

Elaboration

I am truthful with my students and their parents. I am honest in my dealings with other professionals. My students and colleagues are able to depend on me because I consistently do my job to the best of my ability.

Guided Reflections

I model honesty and dependability.

Name three things your students can count on from you.

1. _____
2. _____
3. _____

Name three things your colleagues and your administrator can count on from you.

1. _____
2. _____
3. _____

Name three things the parents of your students can count on from you.

1. _____

2. _____

3. _____

When was the last time you modeled honesty for your students? Describe it.

_____

_____

_____

_____

_____

_____

_____

_____

_____

_____

_____

_____

_____

_____

_____

_____

Affirmation 22

I encourage my students to think.

 Elaboration

My students are thinkers. They are reflective and thoughtful participants in our classroom. I help them understand that their first thought is not always their best thought, so speed is not generally the desired outcome. While some students are thinking carefully, the others practice patience. I increase my wait time to give students the opportunity to think through their responses. I call on someone else only when my student gives me the signal to do so. Then, I let that student choose a classmate to call on for some help. I teach my students about the brain and how it functions. They understand about thinking from the inside out. I encourage them to drink more water, eat healthy food, and get plenty of sleep. I make sure the lesson being taught is relevant and challenging so that it stretches my students' minds into higher levels of thinking.

 Guided Reflections

I encourage my students to think.

List an example of an open-ended question that you asked recently.

_____

_____

_____

_____

_____

_____

_____

Ask another teacher to observe you teach for 10 minutes and record your wait time following each question. Record the average time in seconds here: _____

Are you surprised by the time? Even though you were aware of your wait time, do you think it was long enough for each of your students to reflect on his or her best response? _____

Make a point to learn two new facts about the brain. Then share them with your students as a way to help them understand how learning takes place. List the two facts below.

1. _____

2. _____

If age appropriate, have students record and graph two of these areas: the amount of water they consume in one day, the number of hours of sleep they got in one night, how healthy their food was in one day, the number of hours they watched TV or played video games, or the number of hours they spent on school work while at home. Parents of young children can help with this. Then discuss and post the results.

   Try asking questions that evoke higher-order thinking. Ask your students to evaluate something, to analyze their performance, or to predict an event based on past experience. List two such questions below.

1. _____

2. _____

Affirmation 23

I enjoy the diversity of my students.

§ Elaboration

I love the diversity my students bring to the classroom, and I am continually challenged to meet their unique needs. How boring it would be if all of my students looked exactly alike! I would not be able to tell them apart. If they all learned in the same way and at the same rate, it would save a lot of time, but teaching would become mechanical and boring. My class is a microcosm of the world outside. Because my students learn to get along with each other in the classroom, they are more prepared to accept and enjoy the differences they find in people now and in the future.

⚜ Guided Reflections

I enjoy the diversity of my students.

Think of your two top students and your two weakest students. Describe them.

_____

_____

_____

_____

_____

_____

_____

In what ways do each of these four students contribute to the richness of your classroom?

_____

_____

How does your classroom mirror your community?

_____

_____

How is diversity celebrated in your school?

_____

_____

Do students in your school truly appreciate their differences, or do they see those differences as reasons to distance themselves from one another?

_____

_____

List members of the community who might help with this. (Be creative here.)

_____

_____

List the things that you personally enjoy with respect to the diversity of your group.

_____

_____

Affirmation 24

*I share positive moments from my
class with colleagues.*

Elaboration

*I know all too well that teaching is a very difficult job. For some
educators, unfortunately, teaching can be lonely and unfulfilling.
With this reality in mind, I refrain from complaining in the
teachers' lounge or lunchroom even when I am having a terrible
day. (Yes, it happens to all of us.) Instead, I find a positive moment
and share it with a colleague. I am in the habit of asking others to
share their good news about students with me as well. This upbeat
sharing brings us joy and often laughter, which transforms
difficult days into pleasant ones.*

⚜ Guided Reflections

I share positive moments from my class with colleagues.

Think of the other teachers with whom you work. Is there someone
who might benefit from a cheerful story that you could supply?
_____ If so, jot down a few ideas that might put a
smile into that teacher's day.

_____

_____

_____

_____

_____

Sometimes we are uncomfortable sharing positive stories with other teachers because it feels like bragging. Strive to move beyond this perception by routinely and intentionally bringing pleasantness into situations with others. List times and places where you can accomplish this.

_____

_____

_____

_____

_____

_____

_____

_____

Is there someone with whom you work who is going through a difficult personal situation at this time? _____
If so, list ways that you and others can reach out to this individual to help him or her get through this challenging time.

_____

_____

_____

_____

_____

_____

_____

_____

_____

Affirmation 25

*I know how the brain works best, and
I teach accordingly.*

⸖ Elaboration

*I give my students periodic "brain breaks" to provide the time
necessary for them to make personal meaning out of what was just
presented. I know that lecturing to students for long periods of time
actually makes learning harder. I get my student up, moving
around, and actively involved in their own learning.*

*I model and encourage drinking adequate amounts of water
throughout the school day because I know the brain functions best
when it is adequately hydrated.*

*I sometimes provide music for my students as they complete
various tasks. I also sing with them periodically because I know this
activates many different parts of the brain, which facilitates
learning.*

⚜ Guided Reflections

I know how the brain works best, and I teach accordingly.

Think of ways you can build in "brain breaks" for your students.
(These are times following instruction when children *do* something
with the knowledge that was just presented so that they can make
personal meaning of their own.)

_____

_____

_____

_____

Think of situations when you could use music in your classroom. Consider times of transition, independent work, teamwork, celebrations, and the beginning and ending of class. List those situations here.

_____

_____

_____

_____

_____

_____

List some of the music you might use for each occasion.

_____

_____

_____

_____

_____

_____

_____

Plan an activity with your class that teaches them more about how their brains work. Describe it below.

_____

_____

_____

_____

_____

_____

_____

Affirmation 26

I make personal connections with my students.

Elaboration

Students learn easily when they feel connected to their teacher. I facilitate good relationships in many ways. I send students postcards at the end of the summer to introduce myself and plant the seed that this will be a fantastic year. I make sure to learn and use their names right away. I use eye contact, smiles, and thumbs-up gestures and reach out personally to my students. I make a point to learn something unique about each one. This knowledge may involve their family, talents, interests, past experiences, or extracurricular activities. When I treat students in this way, we establish a bond, and our discussions become pleasant and comfortable. My students know I am approachable.

Guided Reflections

I make personal connections with my students.

List some of the personal connections you have made with your students.

_____

_____

_____

_____

_____

_____

Name a unique routine that has become a tradition in your classroom.

_____

_____

_____

_____

_____

_____

_____

Think of one new way you can connect with your students that will build an even stronger bond between you and them.

_____

_____

_____

_____

_____

_____

_____

Are you approachable to your students? _____

How do they know this? When can they speak with you privately on important or personal matters? What's the procedure for doing this?

_____

_____

_____

_____

_____

_____

_____

Affirmation 27

I help my students make personal connections to what they study.

 Elaboration

I help my students make personal connections to what they study so they understand its relevance. Learning does not happen in isolation. Everything we comprehend is tied to something we already understand. We share prior knowledge about the topic. Then, we analyze how this new learning relates to them, their lives, their class, their community, their state, their nation, and their world. To their amazement, we make links from new vocabulary to words they already know. We study the past and discuss current news by relating those events to their lives. In this way, students appreciate that they are part of a much larger world and they understand that everything they do and fail to do affects others.

 Guided Reflections

I help my students make personal connections to what they study.

Consider a lesson you are about to present. In what new ways can you connect to, and build upon, your students' prior knowledge of the subject or topic?

_____

_____

_____

_____

_____

List ways you will make this lesson *relevant* to your students in these areas:

To themselves personally

_____

_____

_____

To their classmates

_____

_____

_____

To their families and their community

_____

_____

_____

What can you do to make one of your upcoming lessons show your students that they are a part of a larger world than they normally think about?

_____

_____

_____

List two creative ways you can help your students understand that their actions (both acceptable and unacceptable) affect others.

_____

_____

_____

Affirmation 28

I incorporate service projects into my teaching.

Elaboration

Children need to be taught to give back to their communities. Their personal focus should be on giving rather than on getting. Regardless of age, children can benefit from participation in projects that are designed to help others. There are many ways that children can learn to make a difference in society. Being a part of an organized effort to assist others teaches the importance of civic responsibility and instills confidence and pride. These experiences establish a pattern of caring that often inspires a lifelong spirit of volunteerism and service to others.

Guided Reflections

I incorporate service projects into my teaching.

If you have included service to others as part of your classroom experience, describe those efforts.

_____

_____

_____

_____

_____

_____

_____

_____

How have your students and their parents responded to this experience?

_____

_____

_____

_____

_____

In what ways can your students reach out to their community to build relationships and provide service to others that you have never done before?

_____

_____

_____

_____

_____

_____

When children are taught to give back, it enhances their lives as much as it benefits others. List some of the values service projects provide to your students, then make a commitment to include at least one during this semester.

_____

_____

_____

_____

_____

_____

Affirmation 29

I welcome change and handle it easily.

 ## Elaboration

The life of a teacher is ever changing. In education, the pendulum of trends, jargon, and "cutting edge" programs constantly swings from one direction to the other . . . and then back again. I am asked to serve on committees, attend meetings; plan school-related events; maintain accurate records; keep the school nurse, psychologist, speech therapist, and principal all apprised of students in need of attention; and find an extra desk for the new student—all while imparting the best education I can provide to each of my students (with different levels of ability, self-control, prior knowledge, and motivation). New challenges come with every new class. The one thing that stays the same in teaching is that it constantly changes. For this reason, I comfortably anticipate change and view it not only as routine, but I welcome it as necessary for growth . . . mine and my students.

 ## Guided Reflections

I welcome change and handle it easily.

List the things that have changed in your life and in your career since you became a teacher.

_____

_____

_____

_____

_____

On a scale of 1 to 5 (with 5 being the highest), how comfortable are you with change at school _____,
at home _____, and with your friends _____?

How do you help students deal with change?

_____

_____

_____

_____

_____

_____

List two things you would like to change about yourself, your students, and your career.

_____

_____

_____

_____

_____

_____

What is the next change you anticipate? What can you do to embrace this change and see it as necessary for growth?

_____

_____

_____

_____

_____

_____

Affirmation 30

*I seek and find peace in my workplace
as I help build a better world.*

∫ Elaboration

*I successfully deal with the many stresses of my job. I stay positive
and happy. I focus my thoughts and attention on what is truly
important about my work, and I remember that what I do makes a
profound difference in the world. Each day I do one positive thing,
big or small, for myself in each of these three categories: People,
Profession, and Personal. For People, I might call a friend I haven't
spoken to in a while, give a compliment to someone, or be a good
listener. For Profession, I might read a journal article I've been
interested in or get a stack of papers graded. For Personal, I will do
something nice for myself like take a walk or listen to my favorite
music. When I accomplish one thing in each of the three "P"
categories each day, I feel balanced, fulfilled, and satisfied. It is then
that I find peace in who I am and what I do.*

⚜ Guided Reflections

I seek and find peace in my workplace as I help build a better world.

Describe ways you successfully deal with stress.

_____

_____

_____

_____

_____

Take the time now to consider how your work actually does change the world! Even when your job may seem thankless at times, remember that your efforts are appreciated and that they significantly contribute to a cooperative and peaceful world. Now, list one way you can do a positive thing in each of the "P" categories today.

People

_____

_____

_____

_____

Profession

_____

_____

_____

_____

Personal

_____

_____

_____

_____

Name one thing you can do to find peace in who you are and what you do.

_____

_____

_____

_____

Affirmation 31

I respect my students, and they respect me.

Elaboration

Discipline becomes manageable when I respect my students and they respect me. Each time I keep my word, it is like receiving a deposit of trust from others in a special bank account. Over time, I build up quite a large holding. When a problem or misunderstanding occurs between me and another person, it is as though that person makes a withdrawal from my account. As long as there have been lots of regular deposits of trust between us, we can withstand a withdrawal—even a fairly large one. Respect allows students to do as we ask, even when they would rather not. Respect allows relationships to endure despite our difficulties. Respect allows me to overlook the shortcomings of others and to focus instead on their worth.

Guided Reflections

I respect my students, and they respect me.

What does respect look like?

_____

_____

_____

_____

_____

What does respect sound like?

_____

_____

What things do you do to establish respect between you and your students and among your students?

_____

_____

Think of someone whose shortcomings have been problematic for you. Now try to focus, instead, on that person's worth. Name at least two things that make that person worthwhile.

1. _____

2. _____

What additional things can you do to increase respect from your students and their parents?

_____

_____

Respect must be mutual. How do you demonstrate your respect for your students?

_____

_____

List three individuals whom you respect and admire, and tell why.

1. _____

2. _____

3. _____

Affirmation 32

My students and I have fun together.

Elaboration

My students and I find something to laugh about every day in my classroom. We consciously develop a sense of humor that filters out many of the problems of the day. School is fun, and my students and I are fortunate enough to realize it.

Guided Reflections

My students and I have fun together.

About how often do you and your students smile and laugh together in an average week? (It might be fun to have a student tally this)
_____.

In what ways can humor add to the climate of your classroom?

_____

_____

_____

_____

_____

_____

_____

Think of a lesson you are planning. How can you incorporate more fun into that instruction and its follow-up activities?

_____

_____

_____

_____

_____

_____

_____

_____

_____

_____

_____

_____

_____

_____

_____

_____

_____

_____

_____

_____

Affirmation 33

My students and I learn together.

 **Elaboration**

> *I learn as much from my students as they learn from me, because teaching is reciprocal. In any given lesson, I shift back and forth repeatedly between teaching and learning.*
>
> *I am incredibly lucky to be a teacher!*

 Guided Reflections

> *My students and I learn together.*

Think of three times in the recent past when you became the student and allowed your students to teach you something. Describe those incidents.

_____

_____

_____

_____

_____

_____

_____

_____

_____

Select four students who could serve as "experts" on various subjects or topics based on their personal experiences, talents, and/or interests. List them.

Students and Topics

1. _____

2. _____

3. _____

4. _____

In what ways can you build units of learning around each of these student "experts" that would allow them to teach others the knowledge they possess?

_____

_____

You have done a lot of important work here, and you put forth great effort and thought into completing this workbook. Your last task is to ponder how incredibly lucky you are to be a teacher. Consider carefully all the aspects of your work and your effects on others and on yourself. List 10 or more reasons why you are incredibly lucky to be a teacher.

1. _____

2. _____

3. _____

4. _____

5. _____

6. _____

7. _____

8. _____

9. _____

10. _____

Your Own Personalized Affirmations

Guidelines for Writing Your Own Affirmations

As you read this book and examine your teaching situations, you will probably think of additional affirmations that you feel would be useful to you. Writing down these affirmations will help you benefit from them. Remember that affirmations are *positive* statements that reflect your own personal commitment to teaching. Each affirmation should be stated in the first person and written in the present tense (even if you aren't doing them yet). Some helpful starting phrases are "I am," "I value," or "I can."

Also, be on the lookout for any negative self-statements that you may catch yourself thinking or saying. Transform them by turning them around to make them positive. For example, if you often hear yourself saying, "I'll never get all of this work finished today," you might write an affirmation that says, "I finish all of my important work." Then, of course, you will need to practice repeating that phrase thoughtfully a number of times throughout the day.

For the second part of creating an affirmation, write out an elaboration that expands your ideas in positive terms by describing what it means to *you*. This process really personalizes the affirmations as you take time to individualize these statements to your own situation.

To write an elaboration for the example affirmation, "I finish all of my important work," you might write about how you break large projects into separate categories and then decide what should be completed right away and what you can deal with later.

Focus on your beliefs and the aspects of teaching you value most. Tap into your emotions as you write each affirmation and elaboration. Emotions activate the brain, stimulate learning, and promote memory. Involving your emotions will also invigorate and refuel you as you dig deeply to find the passion that great teaching is all about. Teaching nourishes the mind and changes the heart for the better, so *always remember that you are incredibly lucky to be a teacher!*

Here are some prompts to help get you started in writing your own personal affirmations and elaborations. Ponder the list of questions below, then select the ones that seem to speak to you at this time. Focus on those and start there. Remember, state your affirmations in positive terms, then explain and expand them in your elaborations.

What are your educational ideals? What truths do you hold dear? In what areas do you want to focus your attention? To what facet of your teaching do you want to give further consideration to strengthen your skills or commitment? Are you happy with the way things are going overall? If not, what needs to be changed? What do you do too much of that detracts from your best performance? What do you do too little of that reduces your teaching effectiveness? What aspects of your teaching do you strive to enhance (discipline, curriculum, technology, innovation, rapport, preparation, time management, leadership, etc.)?

Okay. Now you're ready to go. Good luck on your journey of discovery and growth.

Workspace for Writing Your Own Affirmations and Elaborations

_____

_____

_____

_____

_____

_____

_____

_____

_____

_____

_____

_____

_____

_____

_____

_____

_____

_____

_____

_____

_____

_____

_____

_____

_____

References

Bandura, A. (1997). *Self-Efficacy: The exercise of control.* New York: Freeman.

Blanchard, K., & Shula, D. (2001). *The little book of coaching: Motivating people to be winners.* New York: HarperBusiness.

Brown, T. C. (Winter, 2003). The effect of verbal self-guidance training on collective efficacy and team performance. *Personnel Psychology, 56*(4), 935–964.

Coue, E. (1923). *How to practice suggestion and autosuggestion.* Whitefish, MT: Kessinger.

Dickson, C. B. (2006). Improving the quality of teachers in the classroom. In *ED.gov, US Department of Education.* Retrieved February 21, 2009, from http://www.ed.gov/admins/tchrqual/learn/nclbsummit/dickson/index.html

Dweck, C. S. (2006). *Mindset: The new psychology of success.* New York: Random House.

Foss, L. (Summer, 1995). Animal brain vs. human mind-brain: The dilemma of mind-body medicine. *Advances: The Journal of Mind-Body Health, 11,* 57–70.

Jensen, E. (1998). *Introduction to brain-compatible learning.* San Diego, CA: The Brain Store.

Kamphoff, C. S., Hutson, B., Armudsen, S. A., Scott, A., & Atwood, J. A. (2007). A motivational/empowerment model. *Journal of College Student Retention: Research, Theory, and Practice, 8*(4), 397–412.

Martin, K. A., & Hall, C. R. (1995). Using mental imagery to enhance intrinsic motivation. *Journal of Sport and Exercise Psychology, 17*(1), 54–69.

Palisi, A. T. (1992). Self-esteem and couples counseling. *Family Letter, 12*(4), 5.

Pavio, A. (1985). Cognitive and motivational functions of imagery in human performance. *Journal of Applied Sports Science, 10,* 22–28.

Peale, N. V. (1996). *The power of positive thinking.* New York: Fawcett Columbine.

Peterson, J. (2005). Understanding fibromyalgia and its treatment options. *NP: The Nurse Practitioner, The American Journal of Primary Health Care, 30*(1), 48–55.

Plessinger, A. (2008). The effects of mental imagery on athletic performance. The Mental Edge. From www.library.vanderbilt.edu/

Power-Of-Imagination. (2007). New Westsminster, BC, Canada: Prime. Retrieved February 23, 2009, from http://enchantedmind.com/html/creativity/techniques/power_of_imagination.html

Roure, R., Collet C., Deschaumes-Molinaro C., Dittmar A., Rada H., Delhomme G., et al. (1998). Autonomic nervous system responses correlate with mental rehearsal in volleyball training. *European Journal of Applied Physiology and Occupational Physiology, 78*(2), 99–108.

Spiegel, D. (1991). A psychological intervention and survival time of patients with metastatic breast cancer. *Advances: The Journal of Mind-Body Health, 7,* 3.

Smith T., & Ingersoll, R. (2003). The wrong solutions to the teacher shortage. *Educational Leadership, 60,* 30–33.

Thoreau, H. D. (1985). *Walden, or life in the woods: Oxford world's classics.* New York: Avenel Books. (Original work published 1854)

Wikipedia, the free encyclopedia. (n.d.). Positive mental attitude. Retrieved February 21, 2009, from http://en.wikipedia.org/wiki/Positive_mental_attitude

Additional Reading

Bloch, D. (1993). *Positive self-talk for children: Teaching self-esteem through affirmations: A guide for parents, teachers, and counselors.* New York: Bantam.

Other Works by Louise A. Chickie-Wolfe

Harvey, V. S., & Chickie-Wolfe, L. A. (2007). *Fostering independent learning: Practical strategies to promote student success.* New York: Guilford.

Harvey, V. S., & Chickie-Wolfe, L. A. (2008). Teaching study skills. In A. Thomas & J. Grimes, (Eds.), *Best practices in school psychology V: Vol. 4.* (69), 1121–1136. Bethesda, MD: National Association of School Psychologists.

CORWIN

A SAGE Company

The Corwin logo—a raven striding across an open book—represents the union of courage and learning. Corwin is committed to improving education for all learners by publishing books and other professional development resources for those serving the field of PreK–12 education. By providing practical, hands-on materials, Corwin continues to carry out the promise of its motto: **"Helping Educators Do Their Work Better."**

Printed in the United States
By Bookmasters